GRADE 6

6A   To sing and then play from memory a short melody played twice by the examiner. T
will first be sounded and named. The examiner will then play the melody a third t
required to play the melody on an instrument of his/her choice. The examiner will choo
the instrument.

6B1   The candidate may choose: (1) to transpose at sight on the chosen instrument a melody no longer than eight bars up
or down a tone or semitone. A key suitable for the candidate's instrument will be given.

6B2   **or** (2) to sing at sight the lower part of a passage no longer than eight bars while the examiner plays the upper part.
The key-chord and starting note will first be sounded and named, and the pulse indicated.

© 1989 and 1997 by The Associated Board of the Royal Schools of Music

AB 2620

6C To sing or play at sight, at the choice of the candidate, a melody including the realization of dynamics, simple ornamentation (except when the test is sung) and the more common marks of expression. Candidates will be allowed a preliminary attempt before being assessed. The key-chord and starting note will first be sounded if the test is sung, and words will be provided but need not be used.

Specimen Tests

PRACTICAL MUSICIANSHIP

BOOK II: Grades 6-8
(including the tests for Section 2 of
the Advanced Certificate)

revised edition

THE ASSOCIATED BOARD OF
THE ROYAL SCHOOLS OF MUSIC

INTRODUCTION

The Practical Musicianship syllabus has been designed to cover all grades and to apply to all instrumentalists and singers.

Candidates may use any instrument or instruments of their own choice, providing they are included in the current range of subjects offered in the Board's syllabuses.

Where applicable, tests will be played by the examiner on the piano.

Candidates may, where appropriate, sing tests on 'lah' or any other vowel sound or to sol-fa as they prefer.

Specimens of the tests used in Section 2 of the Advanced Certificate may be found as Tests A, B and D of Grade 8.

Musicianship in Practice, Book III, by Ronald Smith, is published by the Associated Board and offers a number of additional practice tests for each of the tests in the Practical Musicianship examinations Grades 6-8, as well as useful preparatory information and exercises. The book is issued with both teacher's and pupil's copies combined and with the pupil's copy also available separately.

6D1 The candidate may choose: (1) to improvise with voice or instrument, at the choice of the candidate, an extension to a melody over an accompaniment played by the examiner. The implied harmonic scheme will be confined to chords of the tonic, dominant, subdominant, supertonic and dominant seventh of major keys of not more than two sharps or two flats. The candidate will be given a part showing the melody in different keys and with different clefs to accommodate the full range of instruments. A second attempt will be allowed. Keyboard candidates should be prepared to play an octave higher than written.

6D2 **or** (2) to improvise at the keyboard an accompaniment to a given melody which will be annotated with chord symbols. The harmonic scheme will be within the limitations stated in Test **6D**1 above. A suggested but optional opening will be provided. The examiner will play the melody, if requested to do so, while the candidate plays the accompaniment, or the candidate may incorporate the melody in the accompaniment. Candidates will be given credit for the effective use of inversions of the chords. A second attempt will be allowed.

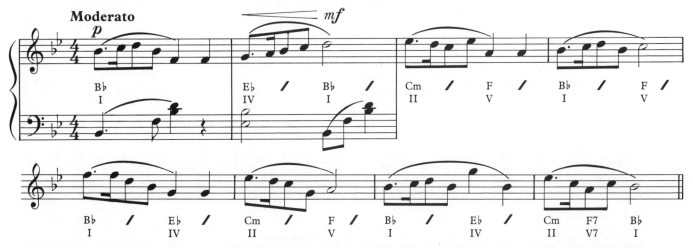

6E To perform a short free improvisation based on a given motif, interval or texture (e.g. flutter-tonguing, tremolo, glissando, vocalization or the use of a specific chord cluster for keyboard players) chosen by the examiner. The examiner will look for imaginative use of the given material, effective use of the voice or instrument and a sense of structure.

AB 2620

6F To recognize, from the printed score, the five changes, which may include pitch, rhythm, dynamics, tempo, articulation and phrasing, in a short piano piece played twice by the examiner. The candidate will be required to point to and explain the differences.

EXAMINER PLAYS

[♩ = c. 72]

Graupner

GRADE 7

7A   To sing and then play from memory a short melody played twice by the examiner, the first time in harmonized form, then by itself. The key-chord and starting note will first be sounded and named. The examiner will then play the melody a third time and the candidate will be required to play the melody on an instrument of his/her choice. The examiner will choose a key and pitch suitable for the instrument. Candidates who choose to play the piano for the examination will be expected to play the melody with the harmonies in outline.

7B1   The candidate may choose: (1) to transpose at sight on the chosen instrument a melody no longer than eight bars up or down any interval up to and including a minor third. A key suitable for the candidate's instrument will be given.

7B2   **or** (2) to sing at sight the middle or lower part of a passage of three-part harmony no longer than twelve bars while the examiner plays the other two parts. The key-chord and starting note will first be sounded and named, and the pulse indicated.

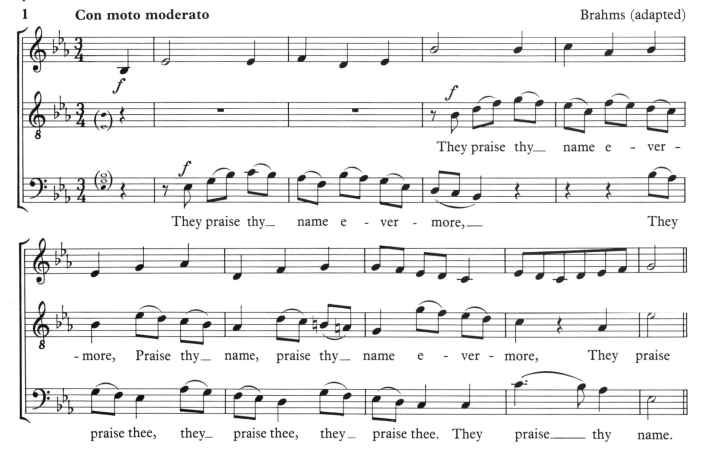

2 **Andante con moto**   Mendelssohn

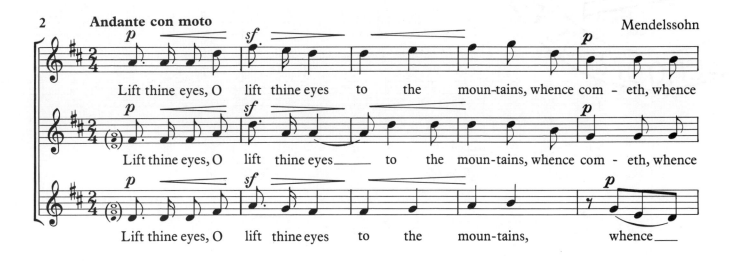

Lift thine eyes, O lift thine eyes to the moun-tains, whence com - eth, whence
Lift thine eyes, O lift thine eyes to the moun-tains, whence com - eth, whence
Lift thine eyes, O lift thine eyes to the moun-tains, whence

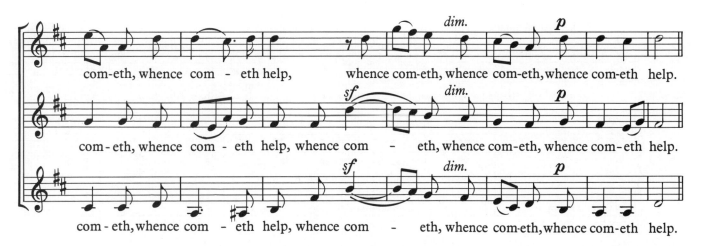

com-eth, whence com - eth help, whence com-eth, whence com-eth,whence com-eth help.
com-eth, whence com - eth help, whence com - eth, whence com-eth, whence com-eth help.
com - eth,whence com - eth help, whence com - eth, whence com-eth,whence com-eth help.

7C To sing or play at sight, at the choice of the candidate, a passage of music including the realization of dynamics, ornamentation (except when the test is sung), marks of expression, articulation and phrasing. Candidates will be allowed a preliminary attempt before being assessed. The key-chord and starting note will first be sounded if the test is sung, and words will be provided but need not be used. The examiner will accompany singers and instrumentalists (other than keyboard players, guitarists and harpists) for the performance.

Haydn (adapted)

1a **Tempo di Minuetto**

1b   **Tempo di Minuetto**

cantabile

2a   **Andante con espressione**

T. Moore (adapted)

'Tis the last rose__ of__ sum-mer Left__ bloo - ming_ a - lone. No__

flow'r of__ her kin - dred, No__ Rose-bud_ is__ nigh *3*_____ To re-

- flect back her blu-shes Or__ give sigh_ for__ sigh.

2b **Andante con espressione**

T. Moore (adapted)

'Tis the last rose— of— sum-mer Left— bloo-ming a - lone. No—

flow'r of— her— kin - dred, No— Rose-bud— is— nigh_____ To re-

-flect back her— blu-shes Or— give sigh— for— sigh.

3a **Adagio**

Antoniotti

3b **Adagio**

Antoniotti

3c **Adagio**

Antoniotti

7D1 The candidate may choose: (1) to continue a given two-bar melodic opening, which will be in late 17th- or early 18th-century style, to make eight bars in all. The candidate may opt to sing or play this test. If the test is sung, a key suitable for the candidate's voice will be chosen.

Allegro Handel

1a

Handel

1b

Handel

1c

Allegro

2a

2b

2c

7D2 or (2) to realize a short figured bass passage at the keyboard. Chords will be limited to $\frac{5}{3}$, $\frac{6}{3}$, $\frac{6}{4}$ and $\frac{7}{5}$ in any major or minor key up to and including two sharps or two flats.

7E To perform a short free improvisation based on a given poem using voice or instrument. Candidates whose first language is not English may choose to base their improvisation on a given reproduction of a painting. The improvisation should last not longer than two minutes, and will be assessed for its relevance to the mood of the poem (or painting) and for its musical structure. Candidates who opt to sing this test may choose whether or not to use the words.

A Song

A Widow bird sat mourning for her love
Upon a wintry bough;
The frozen wind crept on above,
The freezing stream below.
There was no leaf upon the forest bare,
No flower upon the ground.
And little motion in the air
Except the mill-wheel's sound.
Shelley

How doth the little crocodile

How doth the little crocodile
    Improve his shining tail,
And pour the waters of the Nile
    On every golden scale!

How cheerfully he seems to grin,
    How neatly spreads his claws,
And welcomes little fishes in
    With gently smiling jaws!
Lewis Carroll

7F   To answer basic questions about an extract from a score provided by the examiner of a chamber work written between 1700 and 1850 for not more than four players. Questions may refer to keys, harmonic framework, instrumentation, style and structure.

MENUETTO

(i) For what ensemble is this written?

(ii) Describe any outstanding features of the main theme.

(iii) What key is the movement in at the beginning, at the double bar, and in bars 24 and 48?

(iv) Describe what happens in bars 55-58.

(v) Point to examples of: sequence, unison writing, imitation between parts.

(vi) Estimate the period of the piece and name the likely composer.

GRADE 8

8A To sing and then play from memory a short melody played twice by the examiner, the first time in harmonized form, then by itself. The key-chord and starting note will first be sounded and named. The examiner will then play the melody a third time and the candidate will be required to play the melody from memory on an instrument of his/her choice. The examiner will choose a key and pitch suitable for the instrument. Candidates who choose to play the piano for the examination will be expected to play the melody with the harmonies in outline.

8B1 The candidate may choose: (1) to transpose at sight on the chosen instrument a melody no longer than eight bars up or down any interval up to and including a major third. A key suitable for the candidate's instrument will be given.

8B2 **or** (2) to sing at sight the middle or lower part of a passage of a three-part motet while the examiner plays the other two parts. The C (alto) clef may be used. The key-chord and starting note will first be sounded and named, and the pulse indicated.

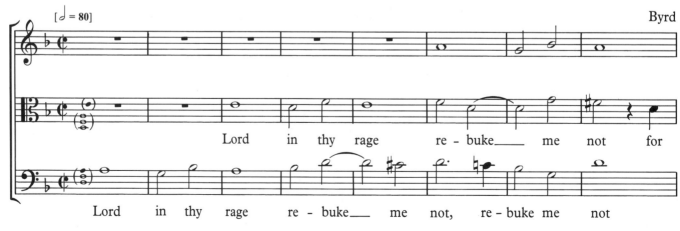

my most___ griev - ous sin, most griev - ous, most griev- ous sin.

for my most___ griev - ous sin.

8C To sing or play at sight, at the choice of the candidate, a passage of music including the realization of dynamics, ornamentation (except when the test is sung), marks of expression, articulation and phrasing. Candidates will be allowed a preliminary attempt before being assessed. The key-chord and starting note will first be sounded if the test is sung, and words will be provided but need not be used. The examiner will accompany singers and instrumentalists (other than keyboard players, guitarists and harpists) for the performance.

3a **Larghetto**

Spohr

Thorns press a - round____thee, Yet, gen - tle flow'r

Smiles still are thine,____ The charm of the bow'r, the

charm,____ *ad lib.* the charm____ of the bow'r.

mf colla voce

3b **Larghetto**

Spohr

Thorns press a - round____thee, Yet, gen - tle flow'r

Smiles still are thine,_____ The charm of the bow'r, the
charm,_____ *ad lib.* the charm_____ of the bow'r.

8D1 The candidate may choose: (1) to continue a given two-bar melodic opening to make eight bars in all. The candidate may opt to sing or play this test.

8D2 or (2) to realize a short figured bass passage at the keyboard. Chords will be limited to $\begin{smallmatrix}5\\3\end{smallmatrix}$, $\begin{smallmatrix}6\\3\end{smallmatrix}$, $\begin{smallmatrix}6\\4\\3\end{smallmatrix}$, $\begin{smallmatrix}7\\5\\3\end{smallmatrix}$, $\begin{smallmatrix}6\\5\\3\end{smallmatrix}$, $\begin{smallmatrix}6\\4\\3\end{smallmatrix}$ and $\begin{smallmatrix}6\\4\\2\end{smallmatrix}$ in any major or minor key up to and including two sharps or two flats.

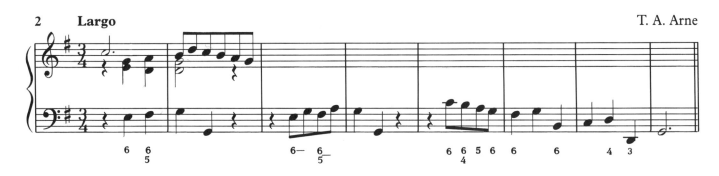

8E To perform a short free improvisation based on a given poem using voice or instrument. Candidates whose first language is not English may choose to base their improvisation on a given reproduction of a painting. The improvisation should last not longer than two minutes, and will be assessed for its relevance to the mood of the poem (or painting) and for its musical structure. Candidates who opt to sing this test may choose whether or not to use the words.

Lines on a Clock in Chester Cathedral

When as a child, I laughed and wept,
    Time crept.
When as a youth, I dreamt and talked,
    Time walked.
When I became a full grown man,
    Time ran.
When older still I daily grew,
    Time flew.
Soon I shall find on travelling on –
    Time gone.
        Henry Twells

Blow, bugle, blow

The splendour falls on castle walls
And snowy summits old in story:
The long light shakes across the lakes,
And the wild cataract leaps in glory.

Blow, bugle, blow, set the wild echoes flying,
Blow, bugle; answer, echoes, dying, dying, dying.
        Tennyson

8F To answer basic questions about an extract from a score provided by the examiner of a work for voice and instruments. Questions may refer to keys, harmonic framework, style, structure and aspects of the use of the voice or instruments.

(i) Name the instruments used.

(ii) Do all play at concert pitch?

(iii) Point out the following: florid vocal writing, angular vocal writing, triple stopping.

(iv) Is this extract from a sacred or secular piece?

(v) Estimate the period of the piece and name the likely composer.

AB 2620

Processed and printed by
Halstan & Co. Ltd., Amersham, Bucks., England

PRACTICAL MUSICIANSHIP
SPECIMEN TESTS, BOOK II, GRADES 6-8

This is a revised edition of the previous book of specimen tests for Grades 6-8 (D 418 5). While all of the tests from that book are reprinted here, the opportunity has been taken to provide additional transpositions of some of the tests for bass or alto clef, and a number of new tests have also been added. Players of transposing instruments will find versions of relevant tests suitable for their own instrument given in *Musicianship in Practice*, Book III, published by the Associated Board; this book also provides many additional practice tests for all parts of the higher grade Practical Musicianship examinations.

Specimens of the tests used in Section 2 of the Advanced Certificate may be found as Tests A, B and D of Grade 8.

A·B·R·S·M
PUBLISHING

**The Associated Board of
the Royal Schools of Music
(Publishing) Limited**

14 Bedford Square
London WC1B 3JG
United Kingdom

ISBN 1-85472-991-8

9 781854 729910

PIANOS · BRASS · WOODWIND
PERCUSSION · STRING

01209 714353

Specimen Test Practical Musicianship 6-8
MK0155   £2.25